ALERT, AWARE, ATTENTIVE
ADVENT REFLECTIONS

BY JOHN CULLEN

This book is dedicated to
THE SISTERS OF NAZARETH
who act justly, love mercy and walk humbly with God (Micah 6:8)

First published in 2020 by Messenger Publications

The right of John Cullen to be identified as the
author of the Work has been asserted by him in accordance with the
Copyright and Related Rights Act, 2000.

ISBN: 9781788122887

Scripture quotations are from several versions, including the New
Revised Standard Version which is used by permission.
All rights reserved worldwide.

Designed by Messenger Publications Design Department
Typeset in Times New Roman and Stevens Tilting Pro Wolf
Printed by Johnswood Press Limited

Messenger Publications,
37 Lower Place, Dublin D02 E5V0, Ireland
www.messenger.ie

INTRODUCTION

We all have memories that are vivid and have an impact on us. One haunting memory I have is of a routine walk through a school playground; a child asked me, 'Father, can I ask you a question?' I said, 'Yes, of course, anything'. Then he asked me, 'Is it true that Santa Claus is not real?' I side-stepped the question, but I could see in his eyes that he was determined to get an answer. I explained about Saint Nicholas and that Santa represented him.

Then a startling question of clarification followed. It was like an *ex cathedra* statement. 'So there is no real Santa that manages to come down a smoked chimney full of soot and yet appears with a white beard? Well, what do you say?' He was looking for real answers of proof.

Like all adults I fudged and fumbled a vague answer. Then he asked me a major question, 'Father, what age then do they tell us that there is no God, just like there is no Santa?' I felt dim witted and flummoxed. The bell rang, playtime was over and I never got around to answering his vital and honest question even to this day.

Advent is an awareness time to help us *not* to miss the signs of God's presence. Awareness is inseparable from the expectancy that was in the question posed to me in the school playground. We look at one another as believers with hope and expectancy.

Awareness and expectancy are central to Advent. Every day we watch the world in which we live and the people we meet with a sense of expectancy. Advent invites us to listen for the Word to come alive for us in Scripture and to ask the Spirit to bless our awareness through the signs of the sacraments.

These Advent reflections help us to celebrate the truth of 'God-with-us', who, despite the lurking questions in the playground of our hearts, invites us in the words of the gospel 'to listen, to know and to follow' (John 10:27).

FIRST SUNDAY OF ADVENT

'God is faithful; by him you were called into the fellowship of his Son, Jesus Christ our Lord.'
(1 Corinthians 1:9)

THIS great line from today's second reading is a good first step into our Advent journey. The Bible is a detailed record of God's search for us. The first question in Genesis 3:9 from God is addressed to Adam. He is playing his own version of hide and seek in a garden: 'Where are you?' Advent is a time to answer God's question that is addressed to each of us.

In the Gospel, Mary Magdalene is in another garden. She discovers that the risen Lord has found her. She hears her name in a new way and is asked to proclaim the resurrection. She is asked to 'Go and tell' as an apostle to the apostles (John 20:17). How did she hear her name? Was it a gentle whisper? Was it an excited exclamation? Was it in astonishment? Was it a determined declaration?

Saint Augustine (354–420) in his *Confessions* probes his experiences with a restless search for meaning. Here, Augustine gives us a good example of a personal memoir, which we may think is an exclusively modern kind of writing for politicians, celebrities and sports stars alone. None of these, however, focus with detail on what Augustine calls his 'twisted and tangled knottiness'.

> But then unknown to me you caressed my head
> and when you closed my eyes lest they see things that would seduce me,
> I began for a little while to forget myself.
> But what I saw was not seen with the eye of the body.
>
> (*Confessions* 7, 14; translated by Benignus O' Rourke, OSA)

Advent is a graced time to unravel the twisted and tangled threads of the fabric of our own lives. Augustine is illuminated by the light of God that only the inner eye of the heart sees. We light the first candle on the Advent Wreath as a symbol of the kindly light that gives us 'the resolve to run forth to meet Christ' (Today's Collect in the Mass) whose presence dispels our personal and collective winter darkness.

Answer the Advent waiting call now.

MONDAY OF THE FIRST WEEK OF ADVENT: FEAST OF SAINT ANDREW

SAINT Andrew in the Orthodox tradition is revered as *Protokletos*, the first called. I think he would be pleased that the basilica in Rome dedicated in his name is a minor one! He was not into self-promotion! The dome in this basilica has mosaics of Saint Andrew's life. One mosaic depicts an enthusiastic Andrew asking questions with an eagerness to discover more about Jesus. Another depicts Andrew recognising Jesus as the Messiah and then rushing to his brother Peter to share the treasured news with him. Another one portrays Andrew pointing to the boy who had five loaves and two fishes. Today's gospel reading is also represented in mosaic in the basilica. It is the call by Jesus to Peter and Andrew, and James and John to follow him.

The phrase 'at once' is used twice in this gospel story to express the rapid response of these four fishermen to their newfound call. Zebedee, the father of James and John, was left high if not dry facing the tedium of mending fishing nets on his own. Later, in another story, the mother of the Zebedee boys requests heavenly favouritism from Jesus.

Advent is a call to us to respond, to pray, to follow, to imitate, to serve and to listen. Advent invites us to leave the boats of our own securities *at once*. Then 'this Other catches me in every moment, catches me again and again and will complete the work he began' (Fr Luigi Giussani, *In Cammino*, p.193).

'All belong to the same Lord who is rich enough, however many ask his help, for everyone who calls on the name of the Lord will be saved.' This assuring message from Saint Paul's letter to the Romans in the second reading is an Advent encounter. This is echoed by Pope Francis in a letter: 'For me faith is an encounter with Jesus. It was a personal encounter that touched my heart and gave new direction and meaning in my life. Jesus, in fact impacts us, shocks us, renews us' ('letter to a non-believer', 4 September 2013).

Here is an Advent prayer from today's Responsorial Psalm.

Save me in your love.

You hide me in the shelter of your presence.

(Psalm 30:21)

TUESDAY OF THE FIRST WEEK OF ADVENT

'Revealing them to children'
(Luke 10:21)

THIS Gospel is about discovering a truth that is deliberately 'hidden from the learned and the clever and revealed to mere children'. It is an invitation to us to listen to children. Advent is their special time. They teach us about trust, hope, expectancy and a Christmas wish list of gifts that hopefully includes a surprise!

Advent is a time to think of and imagine the wish

lists of the migrant children who are cruelly separated from their parents at border crossings, or the children in war-torn Syria or the children in Yemen. They are oppressed, ravaged, burdened and ignored by the world. I heard a comment from a homeless man in London who said, 'the hungry can smell fresh bread a mile away'.

Jesus calls himself the bread of life. He becomes bread that is broken and shared. The poor and the despised know their need. For them, God is not a theory, a definition or a proof. For them, God is as immediate as bread that sustains stifled spirits and heals bruised bodies.

The sole purpose of the Church's mission is to share the bread of life, to welcome *all* to the table of inclusion, the table of sacrament and sacrifice, the table of healing and hope, the table of communion and celebration. It will be poured out for you and for many, so that we are united together with the Lord.

Advent is a time to prepare our hearts to be conduits of the Lord's gift. Advent calls us to see others differently.

He shall not judge by what his eyes see,
Or decide by what his ears hear,
but with righteousness he shall judge the poor
(Isaiah 11:3–5, First Reading)

He will save the poor when they cry,
And the needy who are helpless.
(Psalm 72:12, Responsorial Psalm)

Lord, in our trials,
grant us your compassionate help.

(Today's Collect from Mass)

WEDNESDAY OF THE FIRST WEEK OF ADVENT

'The Lord will wipe away the tears from every cheek'
(Isaiah 25:8)

WHAT a tender image of God! Isaiah doesn't say that
there will not be tears. He reminds us that the tears will
be wiped away. In every parish community there are
times when tears flow and there are other times when
the tears are silent and unseen. In the daily papers
and on television we read and see tear-stained faces
of anguish that follow stories of tragedy, violence,
heartbreak that are often expressed in searing victim
impact statements.

When Pope Francis visited Albania in 2014, he met
a priest, Fr Ernest Simoni Troshani who had suffered
imprisonment, persecution and eighteen years hard
labour under the brutal Communist regime. After
meeting the priest, Pope Francis wiped tears from his
own eyes. In 2016, the eighty-eight-year-old priest was
created a cardinal to acknowledge the sufferings of
many Albanian Catholics who journeyed through 'the
valley of darkness' (Responsorial Psalm).

Tears are the only response to the question as to
why innocent people suffer. The entire world stopped

when a haunting picture of a three-year-old child, Alan Kurdi, who had been washed ashore on a Turkish beach in 2015, was published. The image trended on social media as 'humanity washed ashore'.

On this feast of Saint Francis Xavier (1506–1552) we remember the solemn words of Pope Francis when he visited Japan last year. The Pope met two survivors of the Hiroshima nuclear attack at the Peace Memorial, Yoshiko Kajimoto and Koji Hosokawa. They were embraced by an eloquent silence, tears and prayers. Pope Francis said evocatively 'the abyss of pain enshrined here may remind us of boundaries that must never be crossed' (29 November 2019). Here is an Advent prayer of hope.

> The disgrace of his people he will take away from
>   all the earth
> (Isaiah 25:8)

THURSDAY OF THE FIRST WEEK OF ADVENT

THIS opening line from today's Collect in the Mass echoes the pleading call for God to rend the heavens and come down (Isaiah 64:1). I remember, as a child, singing the '*Rorate Coeli*' chant at Mass and at Benediction during the Advent season, which is based on Isaiah's words. The *Consolamini* verse of this chant is so evocative and plaintive.

Another Advent hymn that I remember is 'Like the

Dawning of the Morning'. The hymn was written by Fr F W Faber (1814–1863). The first verse is a succinct summary of Advent:

Like the dawning of the morning
on the mountain's golden heights,
like the breaking of the moonbeams
on the gloom of cloudy nights,
like a secret told by angels
getting known upon the earth,
is the mother's expectations
of Messiah's speedy birth.

Advent is a time when, as a Church, we journey together and realise our need for the Lord to save us. It is the same plea of the disciples to a sleeping Jesus on the storm-torn Sea of Galilee: 'Save us Lord we are going down' (Matthew 8:25). We all have our personal storms, where we tend to feel God is asleep in the middle of the messiness and mayhem of our lives. Our Church has been navigating a seemingly endless journey through choppy waters.

Advent celebrates God's power to awaken us, rescues us and saves us. God's outstretched arm is an image throughout the Bible. That outstretched arm is extended and firmly nailed to a cross in a selfless, saving action for the whole world. We pray and proclaim during Mass after the consecration, 'Save us Saviour of the world'. Make it an Advent prayer for you.

Advent reminds us that:
only light drives out darkness,
only forgiveness drives out sin,
 only compassion drives out failure,
only humility drives out pride,
only love drives out hate.

Advent enables us to see the present world as a signpost to a larger reality. Advent gives us a glimpse of a hope amidst the ruins in our lives. Advent anticipates and waits for Christ's return, who pledges a solemn promise to free us from all that corrupts and defaces our personal and collective lives.

FRIDAY OF THE FIRST WEEK OF ADVENT

'Do you believe I am able to do this?' (Matthew 9:28) In today's gospel Jesus addresses two blind men who shout an eager prayer to Jesus begging for pity. He questions the blind men and they respond with their depth of faith. Though they could not physically see Jesus in person, they had an inner eye of the heart that gave them insight and perception despite their world of darkness. 'The Lord is my light and my help' is the Responsorial Psalm today. Advent is a time to recognise and receive this gift.

Blind people were also beggars in the Bible and in the gospel stories. Beggars are visible everywhere in towns and cities. In some European cities they are banned by local laws from shopping areas and centres of tourist attraction. In the Book of Deuteronomy 15:4, it is written as part of the social laws that 'there should be no poor among you'. Jesus says, 'the poor you will have always with you' (Mark 14: 7).

A German artist Johannes Wickert who was born in 1954 paints inspiring works of the widespread begging in the city of Aachen, Germany. It could be London, Dublin or any city in the world. His paintings confront you with a tough and stark reality as he wants to rouse people's conscience.

Etty Hillesum (1914–1943), a Dutch Jewish writer and a victim of the Holocaust in Auschwitz wrote in her diary: 'Time becomes a gift when it has a receiver. When a gift is offered and it is not received it loses its power as gift. The gift may be delivered but the door is closed. Prayer is the practice of opening the door, opening the heart to welcome these gifts' (*Diaries and Letters of Etty Hillesum: An Interrupted life*).

Advent opens a door – it opens the door of our hearts as Jesus shows in the gospel story today. Saint Francis of Assisi (1181–1226) said that 'the poor are human beings who have a deep longing to be seen, known and heard.'

Election campaigns at home, across Europe and in the United States focus on the lack of housing, health issues, migrants and the poor. By playing tawdry politics with such issues, we risks anesthetising and

even censuring our hearts, as well as setting the scene for a total eclipse of the values and ideals of the Gospel.
The meek shall obtain fresh joy in the Lord,
And the neediest people shall exult in the Holy
     One of Israel.
(Isaiah 29:19, Today's First Reading)

SATURDAY OF THE FIRST WEEK OF ADVENT

'Everlasting joy will be on their faces'
(Isaiah 35:10)

LEONARD Cohen's song 'Hallelujah' makes the claim that King David had found a secret chord which, when played, pleased even God. The chorus is just one word 'hallelujah'. It is sung seventeen times after each verse! There have been sixty recordings from diverse singers and groups. In church at weddings I have heard it sung with exquisite expression and interpretation. I have also cringed on hearing it massacred by others. But then, there are so many variable factors such as tempo, performance, style and arrangement.

In Hebrew, the word 'hallelujah' means to rejoice and praise God. It is an Advent song about celebration, mourning, regret and reconciliation. It is about a broken love and a true love remembered and mourned. There is guilt, sin, penance, forgiveness and finding peace in the vicissitudes of brokenness. It is based on 1 Samuel 16:14–23. God's presence meets the dire failures of King Saul and King David as well as even Samson's tragic romances.

Today's Psalm invites us to sing to our God. Isaiah proclaims a prophecy that your God is coming to save us. The gospel has Jesus seeing the people's determined and creative faith as they lower a paralysed man through a roof for healing. Jesus address the man: 'My friend, your sins are forgiven' (Luke 5:20).

God's word offers us a positive Advent message as we complete the First Week of Advent.

Say to all faint hearts
'Courage! Do not be afraid.' …
Everlasting joy will be on their faces,
joy and gladness will go with them.

(Isaiah 35:1–10)

SECOND SUNDAY OF ADVENT

'Here is your God like a shepherd feeding his flock'
(Isaiah 40:11)

THE 1971 musical, *Godspell* opens with God's voice, as spoken by Jesus, declaring 'My name is known: God and King. I am most in majesty, in whom no beginning may be and no end'. In response, John the Baptist then calls the community to order by blowing a shofar, a type of bugle, which is a nice detail to acknowledge the Jewish tradition of calling people together.

The cast then sing 'Prepare Ye the Way of the Lord'.

John the Baptist gives a short sermon. Jesus asks to be baptised, explaining that 'we too will now conform to all that God requires'. The cast sings 'Turn Back O Man', imploring us to change and turn back to God. This opening part of the musical reflects the readings for this second week of Advent.

The 1930s and 1940s world of Frank Mc Court's *Angela's Ashes* is in a sense an Advent wilderness for one family. The personal memoir was written in 1996. In the environment of grinding poverty and squalor in a tenement slum, Angela struggles to hold her family together as financial struggles and chronic alcoholism take their grim toll on many lives.

There is no help from her extended bigoted family. The face of the Church is brutal, apart from the common-sense and sympathetic humanity of a priest who listens to the faltering words of Frank. This is well portrayed in the 1999 film version of the book. The scene of Frank praying as he kneels before the statue of Saint Francis of Assisi gives us a glimpse of hope as he faces so many anguishing experiences.

'Console my people, console them' are the words that 'speak to the heart' in today's First Reading from Isaiah. Angela is the true image of the shepherd holding the lambs of her family close to her breast, as she quietly suffers unimaginable harshness and callous cruelty. This is the line quoted at the beginning of Mark's Gospel today. The prophetic words of the Old Testament are the beginning of the New Testament!

Who consoles you? Who do you console? Who

shepherds you as your life ebbs and flows between desolation and consolation?

MONDAY OF THE SECOND WEEK OF ADVENT

'What are these thoughts you have in your hearts?'
(Matthew 9:4)

THE Jewish-American violinist Itzhak Perlman contracted polio at the age of four. Ever since he has worn metal braces on his legs and walks with crutches, yet he is one of the great virtuosi of our time. A story is told that he once came out on the stage at a concert to play a violin concerto. Laying down his crutches, he placed the violin under his chin and began tuning the instrument when one of the strings broke. The audience saw what happened and thought he would ask for another string or send for another violin. Itzhak signalled to the conductor to begin and he played the entire concerto on three strings. The audience gave him a standing ovation and called on him to speak. What he said, so the story goes, was this: 'Our task is to make music with what remains'. That was a comment on more than a broken violin string. It was also a comment on his paralysis and on all that is broken in life.

Jesus asks a probing question in today's gospel as he faces the narrow-minded rigidity of the Pharisees and scribes. They were ruffled by the healing of a paralysed man whose creative friends opened a roof to lower him 'into the middle of the gathering, in front of Jesus'. The nameless paralysed man represents us all in our own immobility to move forward from crisis, suffering, setbacks and breakdowns. He is carried by people and Jesus 'sees their faith' and takes the fractured discords of the man's life and liberates him.

Advent fine tunes our hearts to listen to the music with what remains in our lives, so that we can serve, listen and prepare, recognising that 'look, our God is coming to save us' (Psalm 84).

Strengthen all weary hearts,
steady all trembling knees
and say to all faint hearts,
'Courage! Do not be afraid'
(Isaiah 35:4–5)

As you run the race of this present life,
may he make you firm in faith,
joyful in hope and active in charity.
(Advent Blessing in the Roman Missal)

TUESDAY OF THE SECOND WEEK OF ADVENT

'Like a shepherd feeding his flock'
(Isaiah 40:11)

THE Roscommon Mart was in lockdown due to the COVID-19 pandemic. It was the first mart to be set up in Connacht in 1950. Seventy years later the mart was relying on the wizardry of online technology for sales. I watched farmers and modern-day shepherds from my computer screen in London!

Today's gospel poses a question: which of you having a hundred sheep and losing one of them would not leave the ninety-nine in the wilderness and go after the one that is lost until he finds it? (Mt 18:12) Which of us, indeed? For many of us would find ourselves wondering if we would, in fact, leave the ninety-nine in Roscommon Mart and go after that lame, lost lamb, which probably would not get a bidding or a decent price.

The story shines a light not just on God's image, but also on our nature as human beings. We are often the ones who moan, complain and grumble when the lost are embraced and placed centre-stage. Grumbling and rejoicing are the two responses that are placed in sharp relief in today's gospel story. God is like the shepherd. He goes on a desperate search for us through the warren of hiding places we have made as escape routes from his love, and rejoices on finding us.

Advent questions are addressed to each one of us: Would we search out the lost, the lapsed and the least? Do we see the shepherd as naive and even time-wasting to go on a futile search? Can you sense the tangible thrill of the father who races to greet his son with a prodigal embrace of love to welcome him home?

We talk about rushing home, making it home on time, arriving home and being home for good. The entire Bible is a story about a people's homecoming to

God. Advent is a journey home from the wilderness. Advent is the space to share our fears, regrets, struggles, questions and doubts to a God who speaks to our hearts (Isaiah 40:2).

God speaks words of consolation, blessing, rejoicing and 'gathers the lambs in his arms, holding them to his breast and leading to their rest the mother ewes' (Isaiah 20:11). This year at the December Roscommon Mart, the lost and found lambs bid the highest price, and were all carried home with great rejoicing!

WEDNESDAY OF THE SECOND WEEK OF ADVENT

*'Those who wait for the Lord
renew their strength'*
(Isaiah 40:31)

I HEARD this story in a Synagogue. A Rabbi prayed to God, 'O Lord, make me holy! Make me like Moses!' Then the Rabbi heard God say back to him, 'Why do I need another Moses? I already have one! But what I need is you!' This story reminds us that God has no need of copies – even copies of his greatest saints. God needs originals, a one-of-a-kind. In short, you and me! We bring God the most joy, when we are the unique individuals we are called to be.

Victor Hugo (1802–1885) is the author of *Les Misérables*. A story of 1488 pages! It was first published in 1862. The musical of the story was staged in 1980 and it is still one of the most popular shows in London. The film version of the story was released in 2012. *Les Misérables* is a maze of characters, emotions, ideas, criminality, compassion, heroism, humility, hope, holiness, forgiveness, friendship, resilience, free will, gentleness, goodness, poverty, pathos, poetry, oppression, tyranny, faith and love that reflect our shared humanity today. Two memorable lines give this story an Advent nuance: 'To love another person is to see the face of God.' 'The supreme happiness of life is the conviction that we are loved.'

A haunting image from the 1862 story that is perfectly merged in the 2012 film version, is the stolen candlesticks that accompany the rescued and redeemed Jean. They are with him as he dies. 'He lay back with his head turned to the skies and the light from the two candlesticks fell upon his face.'

A line from the Entrance Antiphon for today's Mass reads: 'He will illumine what is hidden in the darkness and reveal himself to all nations'. The Advent candles invite us to journey from misery to mercy like the *Les Misérables* story. The two-line gospel has a humble and gentle Jesus inviting us to 'learn from me' and to 'Come to me all you who labour and are overburdened, and I will give you rest' (Matthew 11:28).

The Lord is compassion and love,
slow to anger and rich in mercy.
He does not treat us according to our sins
nor repay us according to our fault.

(Today's Responsorial Psalm)

THURSDAY OF THE SECOND WEEK OF ADVENT

'Before they call I will answer'
(Isaiah 65:24)

IN the early days of rock 'n' roll a unique event happened by accident. Four of the biggest stars at the time happened to be in the same recording studio on Tuesday 4 December 1956. They were Carl Perkins (1932–1998), Johnny Cash (1932–2003), Elvis Presley (1935–1977) and Jerry Lee-Lewis (1935–). They had met to have a 'jam' session. Someone left the tapes rolling and unknown to them their 'jamming' session was accidently recorded and then later released under the title, *Million Dollar Quartet.*

The four singers, when they got together for this impromptu session, sang neither rock 'n' roll nor country and western songs. No, they sang hymns and gospel songs! They had all grown up in Southern Pentecostal Churches that drew on a shared ground of Spirituals, Gospel and the charismatic hymns that broke down the social and religious barriers that fragmented and categorised people. They sang about Advent themes such as the prophets of the Old Testament, the presence of the Holy One in their midst, and God's kingdom on the earth. Rock 'n' roll, the music genre that was once termed 'the devil's music', began with Gospel music! Many of the leading artists of Soul from Ray Charles (1930–2004), Sam Cooke (1931–1964) and Aretha Franklin (1942–2018) to

Diana Ross (1944–) got their start singing in a church choir.

The sermon style of Gospel music appeals to the ear with its improvisation, repetition and dramatic pauses. The act of call-and-response harnesses a relationship between the singer / preacher and the congregation. The song / sermon is not just words written on a page, but a living, breathing creation.

John the Baptist's words are proclaimed at every Mass – 'behold the Lamb of God who takes away the sins of the world' (John 1:29). Advent is our expression of belief in what John the Baptist says about Jesus.

While we may be at a standstill, God does not stand still, but precedes us with his words and deeds and waits patiently for us to listen and to follow.

May we hear the Advent Gospel music
that calls us to believe, to witness and to follow.

FRIDAY OF THE SECOND WEEK OF ADVENT

'O that you had paid attention to my commandments'
(Isaiah 48:18)

WE all have 'if' moments in our lives. *If* only I had not said it. *If* only I had not gone there. *If* only I made a better choice. *If* only I visited them. *If* only I made a better effort to see them. *If* only I listened. *If* only I had more time. *If* only I had spoken up.

Rudyard Kipling (1865–1936) wrote a poem called 'IF' in 1895. It was voted the most popular poem in Britain in the year 2000. The poem poses questions on how to develop the qualities of good character that bring balance to your life. He points out the need to avoid panic and difficult situations, to possess self-confidence but not conceit; to be patient and, in the face of anger and hatred, maintain humility. He encourages dreams and yet calls for realism in the face of triumph and disaster. He describes a readiness to put everything aside even to the point of personal sacrifice for an ideal and inspiring truth that we believe in.

The Old Testament contains many an 'if' from God: *if* you follow, *if* you observe, *if* you turn, *if* you do away with the clenched fist, *if* you understand. The Gospels have many 'if' guides from Jesus: *if* they did not listen to Moses, *if* you bring your gift to the altar, *if* today you listen to his voice, *if* your faith was the size of a mustard seed, *if* only you knew the gift that God is offering you, *if* I your Lord and Master cannot wash your feet.

Advent calls us to a new alertness and awareness. Advent reminds that God speaks gently to us, often without words. Creation provides us with the varied vocabulary of leaves, clouds, water, shafts of light that are not to be found in books. Children teach us the gift of wonder and awe, when they pause in the middle of play activity and become lost in a silent awe of contemplation of some natural object, living creation or picture. They teach us the quality of looking, listening and delighting with eye and ear in the wonders of our common home.

Faith and religion go beyond the admiration of the poet and the philosopher to the 'how' of things and leads us to find the bond linking us with the 'who' – God our Creator.

'Many things have to change course, but it is we human beings above all who have to change.'

Pope Francis, *Laudato Si'*

'Eco before ego.'

Greta Thunberg

SATURDAY OF THE SECOND WEEK OF ADVENT

THE 1981 film *Chariots of Fire* takes its title from today's reading from the Book of Ecclesiasticus. It is based on a true story about two athletes Eric Liddle and Harold Abrahams who competed in the 1924 Paris Olympic Games. Eric was a Scottish missionary and athlete who would not run on a Sunday because it was contrary to his Presbyterian beliefs. Harold had Lithuanian Jewish origins and was ostracised by the establishment. Both men would not compromise on their values. The message of the film is important for our world today in the face of prejudice, racism and bigotry. Two quotations from the film are inspiring for Advent:

'I believe God made me for a purpose. And where does the power come from to see the race to its end? It is a gift from within.' – Eric Liddle

'I am forever in pursuit and I don't even know what I am chasing.' – Harold Abrahams

David Jones (1895–1974) a Welsh poet wrote in one of his last poems, 'A, a, a Domine Deus', 'It is easy to miss him at the turn of a civilisation'. In our multi-technology world, God is easily deleted from our lives. The unusual title of the poem is a reference to the prophet Jeremiah's reluctance to utter the Lord God's name. It explores the 'manifold-lurking places' where God is present, but where we are blinkered and even stone blind to God's presence. It has shades of what the Danish philosopher, Søren Kierkegaard (1813–1885) wrote about the society of his day as being 'tranquilised by trivia'. It is a prophetic statement and can be applied to our own lives today.

Advent invites us to listen to a fiery Elijah, who in his day was not recognised, and to John the Baptist and the Son of Man who will suffer similarly due to an attitude of indifference, mediocrity and apathy.

And we shall never forsake you again:
give us life that we call upon your name.
(Today's Responsorial Psalm)

THIRD SUNDAY OF ADVENT

'Among you stands one who you do not know'
(John 1:26)

THE terms 'multi-faith' and 'multi-cultural' go hand in hand. They are an accurate description of present-day society across our world. The fact is obvious in many cities and towns. A friend of mine who is a parish priest in a north-London suburb, thought it would be a good idea to have the gospel of Pentecost Sunday read in the different languages of his parishioners. He began to count. When he got to forty-five different languages, he abandoned the project! In parts of London the language count is 178. *Among you stands one who you do not know.*

I met a married couple from Nigeria who worked on night duty in Roscommon hospital. One Sunday morning, I was getting ready for the early Mass at 8.15. They came in to talk to me. They were shattered and fatigued. They asked to be excused from the Mass. Then they asked me a startling request, if I would read and explain the Word of God for that particular Sunday. They said that hearing this Word instead of going to Mass, would nourish and sustain them as their prayer for that day. Their hidden witness preached and lived the Gospel for me that day. *Among you stands one who you do not know.*

Advent celebrates our search for meaning, purpose and wholeness. It is succinctly put as our search for

God and, conversely, God's search for us. Our search is led and radically changed by Jesus Christ, born of the Chosen People, who does not merely speak 'in the name of God' but he is God himself speaking his eternal Word made flesh. *Among you stands one who you do not know.*

Our Catholic and Christian faith should not be defined or understood by what it is not. It is not a narrow denomination or a breakaway movement. It is a gifted response to a revealed truth – a truth which possesses it, and not a truth which any Catholic can ever pretend to possess fully. The anguish that has scarred innocent lives in the Church for decades is a painful festering wound. The Church forgot the truth of today's gospel: *among you stands one who you do not know.*

Our Advent journey is about waiting, wonder, welcome, prayer, preparation, penance and promise. Advent celebrates with joy on this rejoicing Sunday that *among you stands one who you do not know.*

MONDAY OF THE THIRD WEEK OF ADVENT

'And they argued with one another'
(Matthew 21:25)

Brendan O'Connor from Sligo was my English teacher. He died earlier this year. He gave me a great love and appreciation of prose and poetry. He saw potential in every student, and this was expressed in the creative writing class that he introduced. I still remember him teaching us about Thomas Malory's (1415–1476) *Le Morte d'Arthur* and asking us to underline one sentence in the prescribed text. It is when the knights of King Arthur say to one another, 'Let us take the adventure that God sends us'. He reminded us to believe that our lives are a gift and an adventure from God. Advent is the first part of the word 'adventure'. We pray our way through this adventure of dark and light, past and future, emptiness and fulfilment, waiting and consolation.

Saint Oscar Romero (1917–1980) had a long Advent of painful waiting as Archbishop of San Salvador. *Sentir con la Iglesia*, 'Feeling with the Church', this was his motto. 'Feeling with the Church' meant more than a glib aspiration or a passive loyalty to teaching and the good order of the Church. It meant for Oscar Romero, sharing the agony of Christ's body and *arguing* (to use today's gospel word) for all who were oppressed and tortured repeatedly by a vicious cycle of violence that was approved by the government and a ruthless army.

'You are the image of the divine victim. You are Christ today, suffering in history.' These words were uttered by Oscar Romero in the town of Aguilares, where soldiers had shot open a tabernacle in the church and left the floor littered with consecrated hosts and then massacred the local people who tried to protect the church from attack. There could be no more powerful a sign of what was going on in terms of the state against the Body of Christ.

On one occasion, when Oscar Romero was returning from abroad, an official at the airport said loudly as he passed, 'there goes the truth'. May all Christians live up to this tribute.

Incline a merciful ear to our cry, O Lord,
and, casting light on the darkness of our hearts,
visit us with the grace of your Son.

(Today's Collect from Mass)

TUESDAY OF THE THIRD WEEK OF ADVENT

*'For I will leave in the midst of you
a people humble and lowly.'*
(Zephaniah 3:12)

THE Advent hymn 'O come, O come Emmanuel' was translated from an eighth-century Latin text by an Anglican priest, John Mason Neale (1818–1866). The line, 'Make safe the way that leads on high and close the path to misery' is both a lens and prayer to chart our Advent journey. It is a perfect summary of the Christian life.

I heard an English politician say in a discussion, 'without a vision the people perish' and then attributing the origin of this to Margaret Thatcher! It is King

Solomon who is the author in the Book of Proverbs 29:18. We had 9/11, the financial recession, the dire effects of austerity, the crisis in the Church following the revelations of child abuse, ISIS, climate change and COVID-19. One question emerges in the discussion of all these crises: who and what are we for? In the analysis of this question we learn that as a society and as a Church we have lost our sense of a collective, shared story. We no longer know who we are, why we are here and what are we trying to become.

The Bible tells a story about a wandering people in exile whose hearts 'go astray' and who 'have not known my [God's] ways' (Hebrews 3:10). They also forgot their shared story. The Church prays this story in the Divine Office every day under the apt title of 'frequently recurring texts'. Sadly, we have become blinkered by an attitude of 'everyman for himself', 'the survival of the fittest' and 'a me-first individualism' that is corrosive. We lost the plot of our shared story.

Our Advent rituals, prayers, traditions, customs, liturgy and worship keep our shared story alive and refreshed. Advent reminds us that we belong together. 'I am my sibling's keeper' even when they fail, betray, deny and falter; even when they are hurt and ashamed.

Advent is a tender forgiveness when the bruised reed of love is crushed violently. Advent offers us a motivation to focus on the values that shape our lives. Advent dares us to look differently and to believe in the prayers, promises and prophecies that God pledges to us. Advent calls us to rediscover, rejoice, revive and

renew our shared story as God's beloved, chosen people.
Advent is a serious time of soul-searching and grace.

O, that today you would listen to his voice.
O come, thou dayspring, come and cheer,
our spirits by thine advent here;
disperse the gloomy clouds of night,
and death's dark shadows put to flight.

('O come, O come Emmanuel')

WEDNESDAY OF THE THIRD WEEK OF ADVENT

*He will illumine what is hidden in the darkness
and reveal himself to all nations.*
(Entrance Antiphon for Today's Mass)

Alfred Lord Tennyson (1809–1892) was a renowned
English poet. In 1833 he began writing a series called
In Memoriam after the death of his close friend Arthur
Henry Hallam. It consists of 131 poems which he
completed in 1850. This was for Tennyson a long
Advent of grief, doubt and despair. We have the
familiar lines from the poem

There lives more faith in honest doubt,
Believe me, than in half creeds.

(*In Memoriam*, XCVI)

The prelude of the poem has a positive message for the
lurking doubts we have today

Our little systems have their day;

They have their day and cease to be:
They are but broken lights of thee.
And thou, O Lord, are more than they.

We have but faith: we cannot know;
For knowledge is of things we see;
And yet we trust it comes from thee,
A beam in darkness: let it grow.

This can be a very hard time of the year for people who have had a death in the family or for others who have experienced loss, like a family break-up, a redundancy, an eviction, a prison sentence. All these people face Christmas for the first time without a family member.

William Blake (1757–1827), another prolific English poet and artist, writes in *Song of Innocence and Experience* about a child who awakens a divine love that transcends prejudice and bigotry

And we are put on this earth a little space
that we may learn to bear the beams of love.

(Song 5)

Blake in Song 18 writes 'All pray in their distress'. This is the common experience of all religions.

And all must love the human form,
In heathen, Turk, or Jew;
Where Mercy, Love and Pity dwell
There God is dwelling too.

(Song 18)

I will hear what the Lord God has to say,
a voice that speaks of peace,
peace for his people.
(Today's Responsorial Psalm)

See Appendix for Thursday and Friday of the Third Week of Advent

17 DECEMBER

'Blessed be his glorious name forever'
(Psalm 72:19)

THE family tree of Jesus is put before us in the opening lines of Matthew's Gospel. It is a long list! The name that stands out is David. Matthew gives Jesus the title 'Son of David' (Matthew 1:1). David is described as 'the King' (Matthew 1:6). Jesus is called 'the Christ' (Matthew 12:16), meaning the anointed one. Matthew proclaims Jesus, not only as the Christ and not only as the one who will save his people from their sins but as Emmanuel – God-with-us.

The 2014 Film *12 Years a Slave* is based on the nineteenth-century memoir of Solomon Northup. He was educated, a carpenter, a musician and a family man from New York State. He was kidnapped and sold into slavery to a Louisiana owner. This was a common and acceptable practice at the time. Solomon was completely stripped of his past, his identity and even had his name changed to Platt.

A name given to him by someone else that also belonged to a runaway slave from Georgia. The name was tied to him like the ropes that bound him and which he could not shake and could not undo. His own name had been thrown away as blithely as you blow away leaves. His family tree had been ruptured and he was made invisible, as if he never existed. It was probably his father's name handed on to his son.

The film is a searing, intense catalogue of cruelty, savagery, violence, flogging and brutal hangings. Solomon has a protracted twelve-year Advent. He exists by inwardly owning his own name, suppressing his rage, pretending he is illiterate and cleverly feigning subservience in order to survive. In the end, he is freed because he does not forget his original family name. Some memorable lines from Solomon are prophetic

What difference is there in the colour of the soul? I could not comprehend the justice of that law or that religion, which upholds or recognises the principle of slavery. Life is dear to everything, the worm that crawls upon the ground will struggle for it.

O God, Creator and Redeemer of human nature, having taken to himself our humanity, may grant us a share in is divinity.
(Collect from Today's Mass)

18 DECEMBER

'He will save his people from their sins'
(Matthew 1:21)

'WHISPERING Hope' is a song that was written in 1868 by Septimus Winner. It is an ideal Advent song about 'hope with a gentle persuasion whispers her comforting word'. The Year of Faith in the words of Pope Benedict was 'a call to an authentic and renewed conversion to the Lord, the one Saviour of the World' (*Porta Fidei*).

These words are an Advent compass for us to find our bearings and 'to lead human beings out of the wilderness in which they find themselves to the place of life and friendship with Christ that gives us life in fullness' (*Porta Fidei*). Pope Benedict's writings and sermons have one focus and it is that 'we are not just thrown up into the world by some quirky evolution. The underlying truth is that each person is meant to exist. Each person is God's own idea.' (*God and the World: Believing and Living in Our Time*).

The seventy-nine-year-old Bob Dylan comes from a tradition of American folk-singers such as Woody Guthrie (1912–1967) for whom the journey and the documenting of his experience of life is the main ingredient of his music and composition. In 'A Hard Rain's A-Gonna Fall', he sings about walking through a world which is surreal and unjust and singing what he sees – a newly born baby, lurking wolves, a road made of diamonds with nobody using it, a dark branch dripping blood, a room full of men with blood-stained hammers.

It is his Advent journey to stand with the vulnerable and the voiceless. In the song 'Slow Train Coming', he equates it with the imminent return of Christ and calls on human beings to wake up. Similarly, in 'The Groom's Still Waiting at the Altar', he sees the groom as Christ, who awaits his bride – the Church – to return and arise from their slumber.

Each of us is the result
of a thought of God.
Each of us is willed.
Each of us is necessary.
Each of us is loved.

(Pope Benedict 24 April 2005, Mass of his inauguration)

19 DECEMBER

'Do not be afraid, Zechariah,
for your prayer has been heard'
(Luke 1:13)

MARTIN Luther King (1929–1968) was an activist, spokesperson and leader of the Civil rights Movement from 1958 until he was assassinated. He was awarded the Nobel Peace Prize in 1964 for promoting racial justice through non-violence and lawful civil disobedience. He was motivated by his Christian beliefs and by Mahatma Gandhi (1869–1948).

Martin Luther King is an Advent voice today for the excluded and exploited across our world. He is an inspiring champion for the homeless, the undocumented, the low-skilled migrant, who is told there is no room for them. The term 'low-skilled' is written into legislation that was recently debated in the British parliament and rushed into law.

Mahatma Gandhi dressed in a home spun cloth called a *dhoti* to dress in solidarity with the poor of India in their struggle for freedom and human rights. But we forget that it is those same rejected, low-skilled workers who pick the cotton for the sheets on our bed; it is low-skilled workers who construct our mattresses in factories of dubious work conditions. It is those same low-skilled who stoop for hours in the searing heat of the sun for the tea and coffee that we drink from our cups. Low-skilled workers extract from mines the elements that constitute our mobile phones. It was Mahatma Gandhi who said 'An eye for an eye ends up making the whole world blind'. When Gandhi returned to India after twenty turbulent years in South Africa, he decided that 'Lead, kindly Light' would be the motto of the independence movement. Advent invites us to a new way of seeing, a new way of living, a new way of relating and a new way of discipleship.

Our Advent God is always in solidarity with those who suffer unjustly. Our Advent God is not contactless, like our credit cards! He is a God who makes contact and connects fully with our human nature. Our Advent God is not remote controlled, like the technological appliances that we use today.

John Henry Newman preached in a sermon in 1857 that 'we confess in a God who has the incomprehensible power of even making himself weak'. He is a God who does not sit on a throne, but is born in abject poverty, and who dies on a cross and is buried in a borrowed tomb.

20 DECEMBER: FOURTH SUNDAY OF ADVENT

'For nothing will be impossible with God.'
(Luke 1:37)

BRENDAN Rodgers is from Ballymena, County Antrim. He is a former player and coach of several football teams in the past including as a manager for Watford, Reading, Swansea, Liverpool and Celtic. He is the present manager of Leicester Football Club. In the notes of the match programme he always signs off with his characteristic three-word quip: 'Everything is possible'. In one message of his I read, 'I've always said that you can live without water for a few days, but you can't live a second without hope.'

A woman once said to me, 'I am living with constant tension in my home. I wait in hope for tender looks. All I have is a God who weeps.' Advent is a time to believe and hope in a God who walks in and stays with the brokenness of our lives. The Gospel is a record of how Jesus enters into the darkness, like the seed growing in the ground, like a God who weeps, so that he can be the living, real presence for others who live with the emotional, spiritual and physical brokenness. In the Gospel, Jesus claims that he is the light that is uncontainable that extinguishes the darkness of loneliness, rejection, alienation and indifference.

In the Greek Orthodox Liturgy, when the bread and wine have been prepared and consecrated, the priest lifts them up and says, 'Holy things for the holy people – *ta hagioi tois hagiois* – Holy things for the holy people'. The entire congregation replies, 'One is holy, One is Lord Jesus Christ, to the glory of God the Father'. We have a similar payer in the Catholic liturgy of the Mass.

Brother Roger (1915–2005) founded an ecumenical monastery in Taizé as a place of prayer, contemplation, fraternity, welcome and peace. Reflect on his words:

In each person there is a portion of solitude which no human intimacy can ever fill. Yet you are never alone. Christ is waiting for you and what you never dared hope for will spring to life.

(Brother Roger of Taizé)

For us and for our salvation
he came down from heaven,
and by the Holy Spirit was incarnate of the Virgin Mary
and became man.

(The Nicene Creed)

21 DECEMBER

'Let me hear your voice'
(Song of Solomon 2:14)

MATT and Julia were married for sixty-five years. They lived in and out of the pockets of each other's hearts. They did not have any children. Their friendship was rock solid. Matt died and Julia found herself on her own for their first time in seventy years. A relative gave her a gift of a goldfish and when I asked Julia what this meant to her, she said, 'well, it is another heartbeat in the house again'.

'Let me hear your voice' is from the Song of Songs. It is the only book in the Bible that does not mention God. Yet it is full of imagery about God's searching and desiring and our response. People like Matt and Julia as well as many other couples find through their own friendship and love a window that glimpses God's love. It is the route that most people experience on life's journey.

The Church in Laodice is reminded that being lukewarm about God's love is unacceptable. 'I know your deeds, that you are neither hot nor cold. I stand at the door and knock. If anyone hears my voice and opens the door, I will come in, sit down and eat with them. Let them hear what the Spirit says to the churches' (Revelation 14:16–22). What is the Spirit saying to the Churches worldwide today? What is the Spirit saying to the Missionary Church and the persecuted Church? What is the Spirit saying to the ecumenical and interfaith religions?

Generations of people were influenced by a rigid spirituality of negative restrictions. It was bereft of humanity and compassion. It deprived them of God's gift of loving intimacy as proclaimed in the Song of Songs. His love for us is the voice that is the greatest love song of all time and eternity.

God's love desires and searches for us to be who we are called to be. Augustine's prayer, 'may I know myself and know you' expresses that if we want to love God, we must know God and know ourselves also. 'Go back to your own heart. Why do you want to go away from yourself?'

As we approach Christmas, we need not wait to open the gifts of God. God is love. God is relationship. God is giving. God is receiving. God is forgiveness. God is compassion. God is Peace. God is Presence. God is like the sea going out and the sea coming back, a love pouring out and a love pouring back and pouring out again, 'for you and for many'.

Everyone needs to be touched by the comfort and attraction of God's saving love, which is mysteriously at work in each person, above and beyond their faults and failings.

(*Evangelii Gaudium*, 44)

22 DECEMBER

'My spirit rejoices in God my Saviour'
(Luke 1:47)

MARY is a Nazareth Sister of over sixty-eight years. Due to failing eyesight she reads her Divine Office (Prayer of the Church) using a magnifying glass. She literally magnifies the Lord!

When Mary, the Mother of Jesus, sings the Magnificat her focus is on praising God. In the Irish language we say, 'mol an óige agus tiocfaidh siad – the young will progress and grow with praise'. Mary forgets herself and praises God. She makes space, provides room and creates a place for God in her heart. She teaches us in these last days of Advent to prepare a way for the Lord in our own lives.

Mary Craig (1929–2020) was a broadcaster, writer, and author of *Blessings*, which told the story of Paul, her son who was born in 1956 with Hurlers Syndrome. Through her book Mary explores the apparent randomness of human suffering and she invites us to accompany the pain and raw emotion that enabled her to inch towards understanding and acceptance. In her own unique way Mary Craig magnifies her son with honour, dignity and a unique love.

In the Magnificat the poor are honoured, the hungry are fed, the lowly are raised and there is a warning to the self-satisfied. Every day we see images of indifference and raw violence shown to the poor that affronts their humanity across our fractured world. Mary's prayer is an integral part of the evening prayer of the Church worldwide and it unites all the Churches.

A magnifying glass is also a burning glass. Mary gives birth to a child who would one day say that he had 'come to cast fire on the earth' (Luke 12:49). We can learn an Advent message from Mary to give God space in our cluttered lives. Then the Spirit will descend into the closed chambers of our hearts in tongues of fire, kindling us with the eternal flame of God's love.

Unlike the Son, the Spirit knows no Ascension but stays in the world to effect 'the continuing Pentecost'.

(*Modern Russian Theology*, Sergius Bulgakov)

Lady, take us by surprise,
dazzle our unseeing eyes.
Show us where true beauty lies
in the kingdom of your Son.
God does not know how to forget us.
(Nazareth Sister Mary)

23 DECEMBER

'What then will this child become?'
(Luke 1:66)

THE birth of John the Baptist was not without its drama for Zechariah and Elizabeth. His birth provoked a lot of comment. WhatsApp would have been deluged with this story by all the locals! It is a story of expectation and excitement. The miracle baby that was longed for by two elderly parents was truly a gift from God.

It is Elizabeth who interrupts the all-male proceedings during the circumcision ceremony to quieten the tongue wagging men about the baby's name! His name is John. The silent Zechariah now finds his voice and has his own say about his son.

Often at a baptism, I steal a look at the parents who are holding their child as the downpour of grace of the baptismal water flows over their child's head in blessing and welcome. There is a look of deep love on the parents' faces that defies all language or superlatives. It echoes the question in the gospel: 'What then will this child become?'

John the Baptist turns out to be the man who would echo Isaiah words (Isaiah 40:5) 'make a path straight' and this is repeated in the Gospels. John calls us to a deeper truthfulness:

Make a path straight for the homeless.

Make a path straight for immigrants.

Make a path straight for the innocent who suffer.

Make a path straight for the lost, the least, the last and the lowest.

Make a path straight for the separated and divorced.

Make a synod path straight for the heart of our Church.

Make a path straight path for inter-faith and inter-Church dialogue and action.

Make a path straight for the lonely elderly.
Make a path straight for the addicts.
Make a path straight for those trapped by
moneylenders.
Make a path straight for those who fear losing their
jobs.
Make a path straight for all those who care about
creation.
Make a path straight for those who fear the
destruction of our common home.

Stretch forth your hand and health restore,
and make us rise and fall no more.
O let your face upon us shine
and fill the world with love divine.
('On Jordan's Bank the Baptist's Cry')

24 DECEMBER

Morning Mass
King David is given assuring words in today's reading
from Samuel. David did not have an easy life. There is
a hint of a 'rags to riches' story about his life. He was
a shepherd boy and he is chosen to become a king. His
story tells us about disasters, deceits and deaths that are
partly of his own making. Other deceits and disasters
were also the result of his enemies, whom he thought
were his friends. David had a time of wandering and
waiting as he spent many days and nights in hiding,

camped out in damp caves and roaming the desert as he pondered all the misfortune that befell him.

His songs, the Psalms, tell us a different story. David's words tell us that he is not alone. He is aware of a loving presence that will sustain him through all his difficulties. His Psalms turn to this presence in his times of triumphs and sadness, knowing that he is completely secure and truly loved.

David reminds us that even before birth, God wraps us in his love, knows us intimately, both the good and the bad, and there is nothing about us that can shock him or turn him away from us. We are held and sustained through our darkest times. In the Prayer of the Church, we pray every week Psalm 139 to remind us of God's intensive care and love for us.

O Lord, you search me and you know me.
You discern my purpose from afar.
For you created my inmost being,
knit me together in my mother's womb.

The song of Zechariah, known as the Benedictus, is prayed every morning in the Prayer of the Church. Zechariah and his wife Elizabeth are Advent people. They longed and waited for a child. The lack of an heir in biblical times was deemed as a curse. Imagine the snide remarks and cruel jibes from the people and the temple priests that this couple, 'who were righteous before God' (Luke 1:6) had to endure. Years of anxious waiting, quiet suffering and dedicated serving in the temple, their prayer is answered with the promise of a child who would be 'great in the sight of the Lord' (Luke 1:15).

Advent is a time to prepare for the new events of God in our lives. Zechariah and Elizabeth were stunned into the new event that God planned for them.

He always showed compassion
for children and for the poor,
for the sick and for sinners,
and he became a neighbour
to the oppressed and the afflicted.

(Preface of Eucharistic Prayer, 'Masses for Various Needs IV')

Christmas Eve

The God of the Bible is a speaking God. 'Then God said, "Let there be light"; and there was light … Then God said, "Let us make humankind" in our image, according to our likeness … male and female he created them' (Gen 1:3–27). By his word God created the world. 'I call you by name' (Isaiah 43:1). God calls each of us by name and repeats it twice: Abraham, Moses, Samuel, Mary, Simon, Saul. God enters into a loving, personal relationship of friendship with each one of us.

God reaches all humanity by becoming one of us. We echo the words of John's Gospel in the Angelus: 'The Word was made flesh and lived (dwelt) among us' (John 1:14). God comes to us as a child. The origin of the word 'child' comes from the Latin '*in fans*' which means speechless. The Word of God is speechless because it is our hearts that God wants to touch. Like Mary and Joseph, we open our arms to welcome this

Child. We reach out to protect him and open our hearts to recognise him as our greatest Christmas gift.

He is born in a stable to identify with all those who have no place to live, 'the Son of man has nowhere to lay his head' (Luke 9:58; Mt 8:20). God is so great that he makes himself a child. God is powerful that he becomes vulnerable. God is so completely different that he makes himself one of us. It is the miracle of the greatness of God's love for us in the bedlam of Bethlehem where there was no room for him.

We become children of God when we recognise him in the Child who comes to us. 'To all who received him, who believed in his name, he gave power to become children of God' (John 1:12).

The child is placed in a manger – a feeding trough for animals. Jesus will say later of himself, 'my food is to do the will of him who sent me' (John 4:34), 'I am the bread of life' (John 6:35).

'*Manger*' is French for: 'to eat'. May our hands and hearts become the manger that welcomes our God of love.

The heart of Christmas is the word 'Emmanuel' – God-with-us. God finds ways of being with us always.

> And our eyes at last shall see Him
> through His own redeeming love,
> for that Child so dear and gentle
> is our Lord in heaven above.
> And He leads His people on
> to the place where He has gone.

('Once in Royal David's City')

25 DECEMBER: CHRISTMAS DAY

'Not only does human mortality receive unending honour but by this wondrous union we, too, are made eternal'
(Preface III of the Nativity of the Lord)

HAVE you held a newborn baby in your arms and not been overwhelmed by the miraculous nature of life? Look at those tiny fingers. Look at the tiny toes. Look at the perfect eyelashes. We can all relate to this story because it is also God's story. It is the story of the birth of Jesus – God-with-us – Emmanuel.

Our God is most intimate and is yet, is most unfathomably unknown. This relationship is not transitory for the twelve days of Christmas! It is going to be a reality for the rest of our lives and it will see us through the crisis and the travesty of war, famine and heartache that bruise so many lives. God entrusts himself into our hands – our poor, often unprepared, unworthy, virus-contaminated hands – to become mangers of God in our world.

Christmas changes the way we see the world. Christmas says that God will be present with the lonely, the homeless, the hopeless, the helpless and the broken in the risky danger of a birth in a stable and in the bewildering joys of vagrant and nameless shepherds.

This is a God who is our Saviour and reaches out for our friendship! He is the most precious gift in the world who needs each of us to keep his love alive. We – like Mary and Joseph – are not going to be defined by power, possessions, position or prestige. We are human because of the way we live, love and serve one another. As bearers of the Christ-child, we learn compassion, forgiveness, kindness and the sheer recklessness of God's love.

Brother Christian de Chergé, a Trappist monk, was martyred by extremists in Algeria in 1996. Here is part of his Christmas sermon. 'We welcome the one who was born for us, absolutely helpless and already so threatened. Day by day, we discover that to which Christ beckons us. We are called to allow the child of God to be embodied in our lives and what is more, to recognise the child of God embodied in the lives of others.'

This is the meaning of the bread and wine, the body and blood that we receive in our Christmas Eucharist. And each day, simply, humbly, profoundly and practically, we go on doing this, especially in empty isolated churches. We are called to make Christ present in our streets, in our work places and in all our relationships. Let us live and love the mystery of Emmanuel – God-with-us. This is the true and real meaning of a happy Christmas.

May God fill your minds with the gladness he gives
and make you heralds of his Gospel.

(Solemn Blessing for the Nativity of the Lord)

APPENDIX

Feast of the Immaculate Conception

The first question in the Bible, in the Book of Genesis, is 'Where are you?' This is a good question for us as we journey through Advent. Last January, to mark a special Sunday dedicated to God's Word, Pope Francis compared the Bible to a 'love letter' from God to humanity. Advent is a time for us to read God's love letter. Pope Francis reminds us that God alone knows and loves us fully. His word enters the complex places in our lives. 'Now as then, God wants to visit the very places we think he will never go.'

Francis Thompson (1859–1907) in his 182 line poem, 'The Hound of Heaven', describes how God pursues and follows us eternally. The poem echoes God's question, 'Where are you?'

I fled him down the nights and down the days.
Yet ever and anon a trumpets sound
from the hid battlements of Eternity.

The Koran contains more about Mary than the Bible. The Islamic tradition is effusive in praise of Mary. Mary is the true source of unity between the Christian traditions and world faiths. She is a sign, witness, prophet, believer, model, mentor, mother and the willing receiver of God's grace. She is the one who accompanies, helps, guides and encourages us in our response to God's invitation.

Mary is the embodiment of promise, prophecy and paradox. She is the one whose human freedom to say 'yes' to God, releases the action of God in the world. In a time of confusion about freedom and personal liberty, we can all learn from the trusting example of Mary.

Advent reminds us to look at Mary's unique witness in the gospel. It is here we encounter how Mary was open to God's grace. May Advent lead us to believe that nothing is impossible to God.

Hail Mary full of grace.
Pray for us now and at the hour...
My spirit rejoices in God my Saviour.
Remember O most gracious Virgin Mary.
Inspired by this confidence.
Turn then most gracious Advocate
your eyes of mercy towards us.

When Thursday and Friday of the Third Week of Advent Do Not Fall in 17–24 December

Thursday of the Third Week of Advent
Isaiah calls us to 'enlarge the site of your tent, and let the curtains of our habitations be stretched out' (Isaiah 54:2). The Bible is full of stories about people and tribes branching out on their journey to the Promised Land. God offered Abraham a generous promise, 'for all the land that you see I will give to you and to your offspring forever' (Genesis 13:15).

Advent is an invitation to stretch the tent pegs of our hearts. God does not settle for a little piece of land, spiritual or otherwise. God's word constantly urges us to lift our eyes and see new possibilities and to shake off the ashes and dust that clog our minds and hearts.

Jesus is God's love made visible. He knew that a prophet is without honour in his own hometown. When he did leave home, he hit the road running and he led people to realise the harvest of God's love that is held in their hearts. He chose men and women to help him with the mission and message of God. He spoke from mountain tops and did not whisper his message in valleys. He spoke in temples, where he overturned not just the tables and the money but changed hearts and minds with a radical conversion. He spoke in streets, fields, temples, gardens, at parties and at family meals.

Advertisers are paid vast fortunes of money to pare things down to their essence. Take the Nike advertising campaign for example. All of Nike's factories, sales representatives, costs, energies, analysis, products, projections, profits and purposes were boiled down to three words: *Just do it.*

Isaiah relays for us a core message of the Bible, 'my steadfast love shall not depart from you'. Jesus distilled his message into the love of God 'you shall love the Lord your God with all your heart' and the love of neighbour 'love your neighbour as yourself' (Mark 12:30–31).

Advent offers us a space in the *tent* of our hearts to connect the dots of ordinary goodness. These are everyday gospel signals of people who combine humanity, humour and holiness. In every parish and family we are blessed, anointed and graced by people who witness to a quiet presence of faithful love. They reflect God's love – which never leaves us.

Do not be afraid.

Do not be dismayed.

(Isaiah 50:4)

Friday of the Third Week of Advent

Most of us see the question of immigration as a social, political or economic issue. The place of the stranger and foreigner is central in the bible. It details how God desires us to treat foreigners. Immigrants matter to God. Isaiah is emphatic about this in his words, 'these I will bring to my holy mountain, and make them joyful in my house of prayer' (Isaiah 56:7).

Abraham was a migrant and foraged for food in Egypt. Poverty and hunger are the twins that accompany migrants – even today. Ruth was a migrant. When famine hit her native land of Moab, Ruth follows her mother-in-law Naomi to Israel. A field-owner named Boaz befriends her. Ruth was to become the grandmother of King David.

The Greek word for hospitality is '*philoxenia*', literally, the love of strangers. Its direct opposite is another Greek word, '*xenophobia*', the fear of strangers. The Bible is explicit that by extending hospitality to strangers, we may be entertaining angels unaware. Jesus takes it further. He tells his disciples that by welcoming a stranger they welcome him. Advent invites us to be 'a lamp alight and shining' in the grim darkness of the stranger in our midst.

Parasite is the name of a Korean film that won four Oscars in 2020. It has an Advent theme. It is about rich and poor, friend and foe, greed, discrimination, fraud, fear, hopes, dreams, exquisite beauty, searing pathos, aching pain, the depths of horror, the dizzying heights of fake illusion and utter folly. The film brings you into a world of gasp-inducing depths that lurk beneath the placid surface in the lives of two Seoul families, who live and exist on the opposite ends of the socio-economic spectrum. The film inverts all our assumptions.

There is magnificent, modulated music by Jung Jaeil which moves from sombre piano patterns of the opening, through the mini symphony of 'The Belt of Faith' to the varied mix of choral vocals. The Italian singer Gianni

Morandi sings in the film, in 'Ginocchio Da Te' (Kneeling by you). This is an apt Advent song that has the evocative words – 'I know I have made a mistake. I'll search for your forgiveness'.

Come to our rescue
with the protection of your mercy.

(Prayer over the Offerings)

EPILOGUE

God is soaked
in our world.
God's Spirit
lives and breathes
in and through
all that it is.

We are lost
 only when we
do not understand
that God is already
with and in
each one of us.

Our invitation is
recognition
of God's initiative
to be at home in us.

Then we cannot but
rejoice and be glad.

(John Cullen)